FACING THE FINAL CURTAIN

Donald Gorbach

ISBN:197760126X
ISBN-13: 978-1977601261

"IN THIS WORLD NOTHING CAN BE SAID TO BE CERTAIN, EXCEPT DEATH AND TAXES "

-BENJAMIN FRANKLIN